THE THEATRE OF WOLE SOYINKA

Postmodernism and Postcolonialism

(A critical mini-series)

Kemi Atanda Ilori

Universal Books UK

UNIVERSAL BOOKS UK
Holly Way
LEEDS
LS14 6NF

Published in the United Kingdom by Universal Books UK

www.universalbooksuk.co.uk
Information on this title: www.universalbooksuk.co.uk/ilori

First published 2014

Printed in the United Kingdom

A catalogue record for this publication is available from the British Library

ISBN 978-0-9929618-6-2 Paperback

Acknowledgement
I wish to thank Professors Mick Wallis and Jonathan Pitches, and Dr Tony Gardner, my supervisors at the University of Leeds where this mini-series began as a doctoral research. I wish to thank the University of Ife (now Obafemi Awolowo University) for the opportunity I had in research and teaching at the Department of Dramatic Arts from 1982 until my resignation in 1991.

I wish to thank my students and senior colleagues then and, especially, Professor Wole Soyinka himself, for the great ferment of critical thinking and practice represented within the department at the time. It kept my coals alive for several years when I had to divert from academics to a long and fruitful career in social housing in the UK.

I am, above all, totally indebted to the LORD for His amazing faithfulness.

*Dedicated to the memory of my parents,
Tokunbo (1915-1974) and Ebun (1926-1988)*

Contents

Introduction

This book is the third of a mini-series on the theatre of Wole Soyinka. Although Soyinka is also a renowned poet, novelist, essayist and political activist, nevertheless, when he was awarded the Nobel Prize for Literature in 1986, it was for "fashioning the drama of existence" across his whole piece (Nobel Prize Panel, 1986). Therefore, in a unique sense, what defines Soyinka's authorial signature is his acumen as a dramatist. I employ the word "theatre" rather narrowly, chiefly in reference to the theatricality of Soyinka's dramatic texts – how Soyinka manipulates the constituents of theatrical performance, particularly, the structure and meaning of the aesthetic-symbolic world purveyed in his texts, the iconicity of his characters and the intuitive polysemous language with which he imbues their acts. I will not concern myself with any actual performance of Soyinka's plays. Rather, what I intend to do in this mini-series is to interpret the theatricality of Soyinka's dramatic texts in terms of his deployment of myth and ritual as the core components of his theatrical gest and how these imply traditionalism, modernity, postmodernity and postcoloniality in eight major plays by Soyinka.

The plays selected for this mini-series are: **A Dance of The Forests, Kongi's Harvest, The Road, Death and the King's Horseman, A Play of Giants, The Beatification of Area Boy, From Zia, with Love,** and **The Scourge of Hyacinths**. In these plays, I find an extraordinary mind that conceives the world as a complex of ambiguities, subject to a coterie with outlandish notions of their own identity and place in the world, and ruling a people circumscribed by their proclivities for the abstruse and the abject, as much as by agencies they have failed to understand. Soyinka's plays are scripted for the stage and contain the obvious properties of sound play writing – expressive language, great characterisation, intensive stories, and impressive, symbolic situations. However, in terms of its overall offer, the aesthetics and morality of Soyinka's theatre and the politics of his characters often wind up as Soyinka's method of one-dimensional, single piece attacks on hidebound social and political structures.

Is Postmodernism Post-modernism?

Firstly, the terms "postmodernism" and "post postmodernism" or "metamodernism", "postmodernity" and "metamodernity", and other associated derivatives are all problematic both in terms of their complex historiographies and paradigmatic cultural relativism. They are used with a great deal of slippage and have shifting meanings within the sociology of culture in general, and in critical theory and philosophy (Sim, 2011:5; Bogue, 2002:98-99; Hutcheon, 2002:25; Jameson, 1984:78; Bertens and Natoli, 2002:xii). My use of these terms will reflect this slippage rather than attempt a hard boundary between them. It is also the case that in theory attempts to connect them to particular literary movements and aesthetic styles have been challenged, with some theorists claiming that the literature and drama of diverse authors such as Virginia Woolf, James Joyce, T.S. Elliot, Laurence Sterne, Miguel de Cervantes and even William Shakespeare exhibited postmodern propensities (Hassan, 1987; Caughie, 1991; Moody, 1994:233; Pierce and Voogd, 1996).

However, whilst it is possible to construct a postmodernist aesthetics on the basis of these or other works, I will argue that there are three main approaches to postmodernism/postmodernity as a cultural condition and aesthetic form: (1) the historical approach which breaks European history into three distinct phases – the pre-modern (everything before the Industrial Revolution), the modern (everything subsequent to the Industrial Revolution and until the end of the Second World War in 1945) and the postmodern (everything since 1945); (2) the conceptual approach which treats modernism/modernity and the subsequent "post" prefixes as diffused cultural concepts; and (3) the ideological approach which is essentially part of the discourse on the ontology and epistemology of what is modern, and what is postmodern. All the three approaches overlap as I will demonstrate later, even when the argumentations are sharply polemical and contradictory.

Secondly, these terms are patently Eurocentric, not only in their origin but even more crucially in their application (Cornel, 1993; Dussel, 1993). Non-European societies may have their own pre-modern, modern and post-modern historical stages, but such stages as cultural or historical phases will obviously be qualitatively different in style and form to European culture and history, on the same timeline (Rengger and Mark, 1992; Shohat and Stam, 1994; Dirlik, 1999). Conceptually, therefore, what is describably "postmodern" or "metamodern" in European culture and history may bear little resemblance to contemporaneous instances in non-European societies. However, as I will show afterwards, as diffused cultural concepts and ideological terminologies, it is not exactly far-fetched to apply these terms, broadly, to the African cultural landscape as a result of colonialism and postcolonialism, and as much as to the exemplar plays which are the focus of the present study, on account of Soyinka's prodigious talent and the conscious universalism of his themes and their cultural background (Tiffin, 1988; Appiah, 1991; Simon, 1998; Okafor, 2001).

Thirdly and, finally, it seems to me that as these terms are often exclusively treated as the properties of the cultural ferment that gripped Western Europe, particularly, after the Second World War, and continuing in various stems into the 21st century across the centres of European and North American democracies and capitalist economies, cultures outside of these zones are simply taken as peripheral sites of the postmodern incidental to colonialism, decolonization and postcoloniality (Gutleben, 2002; Crosthwaite, 2009). Most of the discourse on pre-colonial and colonial Africa is framed by European explorers, colonists, mercantilists, exploiters and ethnographers as the exploration and explanation of exoticism, barbarity and primitivism. Perhaps, this supposed immunity of other cultures to the rabid stimulus of the postmodern is one reason why very few studies on Wole Soyinka have actively adopted these terms to describe specific vistas and elements of his theatre, although oblique references are not too indiscernible in the critical and even metacritical parlance of scholars such as Biodun Jeyifo (1996, 2004, 2010),

Wale Oyedele (2004), Christopher Anyokwu (2012) and William Haney (1990).

In this paper, I will examine briefly the cultural and historical claims of postmodernism; I will identify the key characteristics of postmodern drama and theatre; I will then focus on the performative and social practices inlaid within **A Play of Giants (Giants**, 1999) and **The Beatification of Area Boy (Beatification**, 1999). This will challenge the largely critical silence of cultural discourse on postmodernism and the theatre of Soyinka by conceiving postmodernism as a cultural paradigm for describing the society inscribed in **Giants** and **Beatification**, particularly, following the discourse on liminality. In a different paper, I will assess Soyinka's **From Zia, with Love (Zia**, 1999) and **A Scourge of Hyacinths (Hyacinths**, 1999) and their relationship to metamodernism.

Critical Review of the "Postmodern" and Associated Derivatives

Historically, the term postmodern and its derivatives have been attached to the culture that emerged across Europe after the Second World War. More than the First World War, the Second World War was a watershed, a Year Zero event because it shattered the implicit consensus generated by the Age of Reason that had characterised

European civilization up until then as the chassis for the progress of mankind, capable of installing a rational, scientific and industrial method of society everywhere it travelled (Shephard, 2011; Lowe, 2012). The brutalities of the war, its epic scale of destruction, death and disaster reproduced conditions of ancient barbarity and savagery. As a result, Europe became the "dark continent", the new "heart of darkness" where governments and societies desperately struggled to construct meaning out of the carnage of war and the cramped metamorphosis of social values adequate for rebuilding devastated communities (Russell, 1946:492-494; Israel, 2001, 2006; Outram, 1995, 2006).

The dissolution of modernity – the pre-Second World War normative social structure – created a cultural register for society in which the key marker was a continuous and ceaseless search for potential alternatives in every field of human endeavour to sweep away the extensive ruins of the war, replace the old rules and norms implicated in the destructurations of society, and implant a new world in which the prospect of a global war is kept perpetually in check (Haferkamp and Smelser, 1992; Wagner, 2001; MacKay, 2007). Whilst it may sound facetious, the world changed absolutely because of the Second World War and a new world - a total departure from modernity - has been unfolding since 1945, with different seismic points (in terms of jurisprudence, history, politics, economics, technology and culture, particularly).

Although in many respects today's socio-economic environment is far different from the landscape that obtained in the immediate decades after the Second

World War, the broad sweep of history and social phenomena globally remains moored to the liminoid characteristics that came into effect at the end of the Second World War (Wagner, 2008, 2012; Daunton and Rieger, 2001). Post-1945, society continues to be typified at several instances and in different geographical locations by a kind of cultural creativity in which new symbols of meaning, models of sociality and paradigms of discourse take on a deliberate anti-structural tone. The seismic instances vary from Independence and Jihadist movements, the fall of the Iron Curtain and the Berlin Wall, turbulence across capital markets and the recurrent crashes of global financial structures, to tectonic shifts in urbanization, immigration, globalisation, industrialisation and the technologisation of vast areas of social life (Inda and Rosaldo, 2008; Kraidy, 2005; Pieterse, 2003; Castells, 1997; Adas, 1989; Bereano, 1977; Castells, 2009). This is the continuing historical foreground of the term "postmodern" and its associated derivatives.

This kind of foreground is coextensive with the historical paradigm of imperialism that hit Africa beginning in the 1500s (Shillington, 2005, 2012). In other words, if the central thesis of postmodernism is that it was a reaction to or emerged after modernism, then there is some degree of coevality in the intrusion of European domination on the continent of Africa, initially through consensual mercantilism, then the violent Transatlantic slave trade and, eventually, the aggressive colonisation that effected a pattern of conflicted cultural exchange between autochthonous forms of sociality and European traders, occupiers and colonists (Hunt, 2009; Feuer, 1989; Blanken, 2012).

Something "modern" happened at the point of that intrusion – denominated by elements of European technology and industry, cultural taste and political tutelage - that continues to this day to supply and fuel the polemical discourses on postcoloniality. Dating the start of the European colonial period is an imprecise art but the establishment and expansion of colonies which began in the 1500s and continued to the mid-1900s, only ended with the Independence movements of the 1960s and 70s (Ferro, 1997). Four imperial goals have been identified: colonizing, civilizing, converting, and commerce (Ferguson, 2003, 2008). Inscribed in such goals are the evidential premises of European modernism. Instructively, colonialism thus intruded on Africa the cultural paradigm of modernity. The evidence was in the immediate and gradual change to Africa's cultural and social tableaux. In the words of Jürgen Osterhammel (2005):

> Colonialism is a relationship between an indigenous (or forcibly imported) majority and a minority of foreign invaders. The fundamental decisions affecting the lives of the colonized people are made and implemented by the colonial rulers in pursuit of interests that are often defined in a distant metropolis. Rejecting cultural compromises with the colonized population, the colonizers are convinced of their own superiority and their ordained mandate to rule. (Osterhammel, 2005: 15)

As such, the immediate assumptions of colonialism, backed by imperialism, created an image of the colonised as a people and a space over which the enforcement of the preconceived notions of the coloniser as a civilising agency becomes a paramount imperial obligation. This neo-Enlightenment paradigm resolves itself into a form of hegemony in which capital, culture and military coercion became the new universalisms for the maintenance and exploitation of the colonial space and the colonial subject. In Marxist terms, these universalisms are altogether an "instrument of wholesale destruction, dependency and systematic exploitation producing distorted economies, socio-psychological disorientation, massive poverty and neocolonial dependency" (Johnston, et al., 2009).

In an incisive analysis, Walter Rodney (1973) notes:

> The decisiveness of the short period of colonialism and its negative consequences for Africa springs mainly from the fact that Africa lost power. Power is the ultimate determinant in human society, being basic to the relations within any group and between groups…During the centuries of pre-colonial trade, some control over social political and economic life was retained in Africa, in spite of the disadvantageous commerce with Europeans. That little control over internal matters disappeared under colonialism. Colonialism went much further than trade. It meant a

> tendency towards direct appropriation by Europeans of the social institutions within Africa. Africans ceased to set indigenous cultural goals and standards, and lost full command of training young members of the society...It meant the development of Europe as part of the same dialectical process in which Africa was underdeveloped. (Rodney, 1973:224)

This structural or systemic character of colonialism produces categorical effects on both the colonised and the coloniser in a mutually reinforcing dialectical but unequal power relationship at every point of contact between the colonised and the coloniser (Memmi, 2003). Historians such as Catherine Hall (2002), Antoinette Burton (2003) and Mrinalini Sinha (2006) argued separately that imperialism and colonialism could be viewed as cultural projects which moulded the cultures of the colonised and the coloniser in particular ways, especially in the way cultural and scientific knowledge became a shared commodity between the metropolis and the colony. Alan Lester (2001), for instance, illustrates the nature of "imperial networks" through which cultural exchange – albeit in distorted and unequal measures – flowed between the Empire and the colonies.

Tony Ballantyne (2012) describes the "webs of empire" that steered the flow of ideas between the metropolis and the colonies, as well as through the colonies. This traffic also soon became a vehicle for decolonisation in Africa, especially, in the 1950s and 60s, in which a fierce anti-colonial discourse led by theorists such as Fanon,

Césaire and Senghor, focused on how colonialism subordinated the colonised to the distorted cultural and political agenda of the coloniser (Memmi, 2003; Castle, 2001; Barker, Hulme and Iversen, 1994; Williams and Chrisman, 1994; Acheraïou, 2008).

Much of that discourse today finds currency in the works of Edward Said (1978, 2001), Gayatri Chakravorty Spivak (1988, 1998, 1999) and Homi K. Bhabha (2011, 2012, 2013). However, the historiography of the "postmodern" doesn't end with this archival reiteration of its roots. I would also argue that postmodernism and its derivatives are essentially conceptual handles for the cultural and historical changes, happening globally, since 1945.

In my view the conceptual approach construes postmodernity and postmodernism as the cultural landscape that comes after or in reaction to that which is modern (Dunn, 1998; Jencks, 2007). In that sense, one can locate modernity in any cultural zone where there is an identifiable period that can be broadly described as progressive compared to the past, in which a greater latitude for the principles of rationality and hierarchy enables the culture to jump from being merely conservative and traditional to new forms of inquisitiveness, critiquing and a break with the past. The past then becomes either a distant past and is, consequently, fossilized or a recent past, and thereby a focus of constant renovation and re-appraisal, and a point of obvious departure. In a sense, to adopt Habermas's (1990) neologism, modernity becomes a structural vehicle or project for fostering progress based on a break with a form of life that is deemed past, even though not extinct.

As a result, postmodernism is the next stage in that direction of travel in which human progress is, intuitively, both forward-facing and introspective, self-reflexive and antifoundational. It becomes a poststructural and transhistorical phenomenon and, in the words of Umberto Eco, cited by Rosso and Springer (1983), postmodernism is "not a trend to be chronologically defined, but, rather, an ideal category - or better still a *Kunstwollen*, a way of operating We could say that every age has its own post-modern, just as every age has its own form of mannerism…I believe that every age reaches moments of crisis like those described by Nietzsche in the second of the *Untimely Considerations*, on the harmfulness of the study of history. The sense that the past is restricting, smothering, blackmailing us".

In Europe, Fredric Jameson (1991) and David Harvey (1991), for instance, have argued that postmodernism essentially translates into a recurrence of counter-enlightenment ideas, particularly, accompanying "late capitalism" or "flexible accumulation" in which finance capitalism speeds up the mobility of labour and capital across industrial Western democracies. For Giddens (1990), postmodernity describes a kind of social pathology which hankers after changes to institutions and social conditions globally but especially in the West since the 1950s. This pathology is then reflected in postmodernism as a corresponding aesthetic, literary, political and social philosophy, and describes certain decisive shifts in the shape of society, the arts and industry. These shifts are characterised by a continuing fragmentation of authority (or conservatism), the technologisation of the quotidian, and the commoditization of knowledge which social scientists and social critics observe as the ascendant elements of sociality in late 20th and early 21st century life (Shapiro, 1990; Barbeito, 2000; Swan, 2005).

It is this period that is associated, for instance, with Independence movements, the disappearance of European empires, the Campaign for Nuclear Disarmament, the feminist movement, racial equality movements, gay rights movements, the peace movement, Green Peace, anti-globalisation movements, Jihadism and others – and they have all flourished with a clear poststructural or anti structural agenda. It is the period when analogue media with limited bandwidth grew into cable television and an assortment of new media led, originally, by the personal computer and later by several digital means of personal and mass communication. As McLuhan (2001) argues, in this context, postmodernism is, practically, a mass media culture which, in convergence with popular culture, has become embedded in the new Information (or Digital) Age, overshadowing the orthodoxy of traditional views, and pushing beyond modernity by loosening further the authority of normative social standards.

The digital condition of postmodernity along with the idea that culture is constantly contemporaneous and shifting into new forms of sociality deliberately calibrated as a break with some precedent, has led to the newfangled term "post postmodernism", or metamodernism (Wilkie,

2011; Sassower, 2013). Social critics such as Esther Dyson (1997, 1998) and Henry Jenkins (2006a, 2006b) have argued that the convergence of popular culture, the World Wide Web, and media appliances have introduced a spectrum of "participatory culture" in which everything is open to instant change and continuous enculturation. Rooted concepts around morality, authority, knowledge, selfhood, reality and time have been altered by the emergence of new technologies in which the assumed linear relationship between randomness and certitude, order and chaos, the reader and the text, and other modernist binaries is continuously jettisoned (Scholes, 2006; Jenkins, 2005, 2013; Bradshaw and Dettmar, 2008). It is no longer the case that randomness, chaos, anarchy, nihilism, the existentialist angst, amongst other concepts stand merely for negative social principles but that they represent clear cognitive hierarchies of sociality, inherently define new forms of morality, rationality and authority, and ought to be appropriately contextualised and historicised (Baudrillard, 1994; Deleuze, 2005; Slocombe, 2006).

This new view of reality whether we describe it after Nicolas Bourriaud's (2009) "altermodern"; Gilles Lipovetsky's and Sebastien Charles' (2005) "hypermodernity"; Raoul Eshelman's (2000) "performatism"; Robert Samuels' (2010) "automodernity"; or Alan Kirby's (2009) "digimodernism" reflects an expansive social compass in which culture constantly straddles the unknown and seeks to break beyond present horizons in the fields of art and architecture, information technology and the internet, sociology, film, television and literature. As Bourriaud (2009:13-14) argues, "contemporary art gives the impression of being uplifted by an immense wave of displacements, voyages, translations, migrations of objects and beings ... artistic styles and formats must henceforth be regarded from the viewpoint of diaspora, migration and exodus". Perhaps, even more assertively, Foucault (1976) posts this reflection:

> For the last ten or fifteen years, the immense and proliferating criticizability of things, institutions, practices, and discourses; a sort of general feeling that the ground was crumbling beneath our feet, especially in places where it seemed most familiar, most solid, and closest to us, to our bodies, to our everyday gestures. But alongside this crumbling and the astonishing efficacy of discontinuous, particular, and local critiques, the facts were also revealing something... beneath this whole thematic, through it and even within it, we have seen what might be called the insurrection of subjugated knowledges. – (Foucault, 1976 - Society Must be Defended, 7th January 1976, tr. David Macey)

In Africa and Asia, particularly, Foucault's (and then Derrida's) conceptual framework on postmodernism is woven largely into the discourse on postcoloniality, the epic examples of which are the works of Edward Said (1978, 1994, 2002), Homi K. Bhabha (2011, 2012, 2013) and Gayatri Chakravorty Spivak (1988, 1999, 2012). For Said (1978:18), "Orientalism" speaks of the cultural process in which imperialism conceives the Orient as "a place of romance, exotic beings, haunting memories and landscapes, remarkable experiences", within a Eurocentric discourse that valorises the colonised subject and the colonial terrain as the "Other", a wild, inferior and exotic "Other" over whom and through whom imperialism must achieve its self-appointed civilising mandate. But this is not all – Orientalism becomes the operative identity of the colonial subject, a grammar through which he considers himself and others, and a pigeonhole for the totality of his views on life.

In contrast to Said's penchant for theorising the Oriental as someone captured completely within the enclosure of imperialism and seemingly predetermined to follow its script, Homi K. Bhabha (2012), on the other hand, frames the rubrics of postcoloniality around how cultural determinants, especially, in ambivalent ways inform the processes of nationhood, national identity and social agency. Instead of the ironclad binaries of East and West, Self and Other, Bhabha locates postcoloniality within his cultural constructs of "subaltern", "diaspora", "hybridity", "liminality", and "mimicry". These are terms which he invented or reconstructed to specify how colonial subjects and societies were able to produce a culture that resisted colonialism, subverting its power in the kind of morality and authority it exercised over their lives. These concepts provide Bhabha with the "interrogatory, interstitial space" within which he establishes a form of postcolonial discourse that subverts the Eurocentric "linear narrative of the nation", especially, its "holism of culture and community" and a "fixed horizontal nation-space" (Bhabha, 1994: 3, 145). This kind of discourse veers into "practical Marxist-feminist-deconstructionist" investigation of imperialism in Spivak's critical methodology.

Deconstructing Marx's use of the German terms for representation, Spivak (1988) explores the dynamics of race and power involved in the banning of "sati", the social funerary ritual among some Indian communities in which a recently widowed woman would immolate herself on her husband's funeral pyre, by British colonial authorities. In Spivak's view, the accounts of sati in colonial archives suggested that "White men were saving brown women from brown men" (Morton, 2007:113) and completely muted the experiences of the women themselves and the communities they represented. This prompted Spivak to ask, "Can the subaltern speak?" The assumed objectivity and transparency of Western critical discourse in which the encounters between the Empire and the colonial space and subject are foreclosed by Eurocentric parameters of Object/Subject, Self/Other, Civilisation/Primitivism represent for Spivak the kind of "political proxy" and "figurative re-presenting" that Karl Marx adopts in describing the process of inferiorisation and marginalisation of the working classes by the bourgeoisie (Clarke, 2008).

Arguably, for these important strands of postcolonial discourse, if modernism stood for specific forms of morality, rationality and authority, intended as a benign vehicle of civilisation and progress, the arguments of the coloniser to justify the annexation of large foreign states in Africa are mimetic of the Kantian constructs (of rationality, authority and morality, not as something relative but as fixed and absolute) which undergird modernism (Howard, 1981; Banham, 2003, 2006). And, if postmodernism was a rejection of these constructs, and a continuous re-working of counter-Enlightenment ideas, the whole sway of postcolonial discourse is largely bent towards this same end – exposing the false bases of colonialism, mounting attacks on the Eurocentrism that portrays Africa as Europeans had seen the continent, and would like to continue to see it – exotic, inferior, and primitive – in urgent need of European civilisation, capitalism and, ultimately, political and economic control. At various points such arguments both within Eurocentric and anti-Eurocentric methods of discourse would carry the ideological notions of postmodernism as a cultural paradigm.

In my view, the ideological notions of postmodernism are, essentially, about the ontology and epistemology of what is modern, and what is postmodern. In philosophy and critical theory, postmodernity is basically the end of modernity, the grand social project that is construed as a structuralist case (Habermas, 1990; Giddens, 1993; Philip, 1975). Structuralism, in the hands of Ferdinand de Saussure (1959), particularly, had modeled the meaning of reality upon the structure of language. This structure mediates between the concrete reality perceptible to the senses in which humans participate, and the abstract ideas that are used to attach meanings to reality. In mainstream structuralist philosophy, reality consists of several sets of interrelations which have behind them certain morphology efficient and adequate for explaining their discoverable laws (or patterns) (Sturrock, 1979; Assiter, 1984; Deleuze, 2002).

Poststructuralism, particularly, in the works of Jean Baudrillard (1983, 1991, 1994, 2005), rejects this notion of an inherent sufficient structure and the binary oppositions that constitute them, arguing instead that reality is self-referential, that signification and meaning are brought about through an interjunction of different systems of signs. As a result, meaning necessarily becomes plural and relative and the search for more meanings to arrive at some "total" understanding of reality only seduces us towards a "simulated" version of reality – a simulacrum which is a deliberately distorted copy of the real and affects us as a model of truth: the hyperreal (Baudrillard, 1994; Perry, 1998). In its broadest application, this kind of self-referentiality recalls the central thesis of postmodernism and Baudrillard has been credited as an influential figure in denoting the ethic of postmodernism (Kellner, 1994; Hegarty, 2004; Merrin, 2005).

Baudrillard's position is stretched further in the arguments of Jean-Francois Lyotard (1984, 2011) for whom postmodernism represents a constant pursuit of change in which the notion of progress qua progress has become obsolete. For Lyotard, the concepts of rationality and the absolute moral good favoured in Enlightenment discourses are essentially grand projects and narratives which have inherent flaws, and these flaws account for events such as imperialism, Auschwitz and Hiroshima. Consequently, Lyotard describes postmodernism as the collapse of the grand narratives or "metanarratives" of modernism. In his observation, these "metanarratives" as totalising theories eventually cease to command universal consensus in a world in which heterogeneity, difference, diversity, and the irreconcilability of opposing values are denoted as comparative and commonplace. It has been argued by some critics (Benhabib, 1995 and Butler, 1995, for instance) that the debate between universalism and relativism is at the heart of the distinction between modernism and postmodernism, where modernism is held to represent the former and postmodernity the latter.

For others, such as Frederic Jameson (1991):

> It is safest to grasp the concept of the postmodern as an attempt to think the present historically in an age that has forgotten how to think historically in the first place. In that case, it either "expresses" some deeper irrepressible historical impulse (in however distorted a fashion) or effectively "represses" and diverts it, depending on the side of the ambiguity you happen to favor. (Jameson, 1991: ix)

Jameson links "postmodern" and its subsequent theory "postmodernism" as "the cultural logic of late capitalism". Postmodernism or the postmodern consciousness engages sociality as a series of decisive breaks with the past, often denying the possibility of continuities or only grudgingly accounting for them as part of the present narrative act. In this kind of historicity, postmodernism assumes that the "modernization process is complete, and nature is gone for good", argues Jameson, and "a more fully human world than the older one, but one in which "culture" has become a veritable "second nature"" has prevailed (Jameson, 1991: ix). In its alignment with the consumption patterns of capitalism, postmodernism commodifies culture both as a product as well as a form of capital for which currency and recency, rather than continuity and gestation, are the acceptable properties. It is Jameson's view that:

> (T)he frenzy whereby virtually anything in the present is appealed to for testimony as to the latter's uniqueness and radical difference from earlier moments of human time does indeed strike one sometimes as harboring a pathology distinctively autoreferential, as though our utter forgetfulness of the past exhausted itself in the vacant but mesmerized contemplation of a schizophrenic present that is incomparable virtually by definition. (Jameson, 1991: xii)

Jameson's arguments are strong and convincing and directly against any form of historicism that conceives the present as an end in itself. This perceived teleological aspect of postmodernism draws the ire of several social theorists from different critical streams ranging from Terry Eagleton (1996, 2003), Alex Callinicos (1990, 2006), Noam Chomsky (2004, 2006, 2008), and Alan Sokal (1999, 2010) to Jean Bricmont (1998, 1999), for whom postmodernism is a redacted version of endism, or what Eagleton labels "anything-goes-ism". Some reject postmodernism because of its roots in modernism, others because they think it offers merely a re-packaged discourse on the propensities of counter-Enlightenment constructs for rejecting realist epistemology and those Cartesian axioms (completeness, essentiality, uniqueness, exclusivity, and comprehensiveness) underpinning it.

Furthermore, the roots of postmodernism, especially in the poststructuralism of Roland Barthes (1977) and Jacques Derrida (1976), and stems in the psychoanalysis of Jacques Lacan (1988, 2004) and Deleuzean thought in which, paradoxically, the goal of theory is the elimination of theory altogether have also been seen as the source of the mechanistic interest of postmodernist theorists in certain institutional binaries. In particular, the binaries of power/knowledge, Self-determination/Other-determination, universalism/relativism, etc. and the marginalisation of the "Other" in the deconstruction of reality (Eagleton, 1996; Sokal and Bricmont, 1999; Callinicos, 2006; Sokal, 2010; Kul-Want, 2010) have been seen as the weaknesses of postmodernist thought.

Similarly, some contradictions and weaknesses are observable in the polemics of the leading postcolonial theorists. For instance, I will argue that Said's Foucauldian criticism of Western ethnocentrism as a discursive schema for inventing the "Orient" in order to satisfy imperialism and to control the colonial space and subject appears overly deterministic and a caricature of the finer Eurocentric arguments that the Orient is a distinct and unique phenomenon that requires contextualisation and invites comparisons with existing European models (Warraq, 2007; Marrouchi, 2004). Perhaps, a useful comparison or complementary approach is offered by Joseph Needham (Gerstle and Milner, 1985; Needham and Davies, 1990; Ronan, 1995; Dullmayr, 1999). Similarly, Bhabha's postulate that hybridity is both a product of colonialism and a calculated attempt to supplant it by the colonial subject necessitates his theory of the "interstitial perspective" of cultural collision and exchange in which the colonised is almost a consensual agent of the re-modelling and culturally destructive apparatus of the colonial administration. This is quaintly ahistorical and restates in a different way the circular neo-Enlightenment argument of Eurocentric ethnocentric theorists that imperialism (through colonialism) sped up the civilisation of the colonial space and subject (Huddart, 2006; Burkitt, 2012).

The reverse romanticism, even exoticism that this hints of is carefully hidden behind the anti-structural tones of Bhabha. This neo-romanticism is probably more evident in Spivak whose "subaltern" is neither a hybridity or the inhabitant of some "interstitial" space but is the colonised dressed loudly in all the glory of her own cultural accoutrement but dumbfounded, indeed muted, by the overwhelming negative register of colonial discourse, especially, as imbricated in the type of discourse founded on Foucault and Deleuze. In her methodology, the subaltern is not only unable to speak (because she is presented as voiceless by those within the Eurocentric establishment) but Spivak aggrandises the role of this establishment in constructing the identity of the subaltern, and in enabling or limiting her speech-acts.

At the end, the subaltern is not only the victim of Europe's subjective self-reference as the Subject, and its problematic identification of the subaltern as the Other, but this identity is also an outcome of the Derridean deconstruction of the discourse of the Eurocentric theorists by Spivak. Therefore, when Spivak argues that everything is representation, her role is complicit within that discourse and her focus solely on dominant groups excludes the subaltern and the processes she adopts to speak for herself against the overwhelming tide of the mechanics of discourse by both Western theorists and Western-theories-dependent postcolonial theorists, such as Spivak (Sanders, 2006; Morris, 2010; Anderson, 2012).

This overarching polemical scaffold which situates postmodernism essentially as a critical historical and cultural movement sufficiently accounts for its longevity as a form of discourse and its continuity as a rational, systemic, poststructural account of the notion of social progress in both Western and non-Western societies since the end of the Second World War in 1945. I suspect this is essentially due to what I would describe as the paradigmatic cultural relativism of postmodernism, that is, postmodernism as a creative and handy paradigm for reading history, culture and society as interlocked categories and modes of production of knowledge in which the essential criterion is that the thing described relates to the past and the future in a grossly detached method, and conceives itself as morphing, altering and disappearing whilst simultaneously having the effect of being here and unending. This is one way of explaining the kind of universe depicted by playwrights such as August Strindberg, Luigi Pirandello, and Bertolt Brecht who have been acclaimed as embedding in their works certain of the aesthetic codes and themes familiar of postmodernist sensibilities (Travers, 2006; Robinson, 2009; Mariani, 2008; Jernigan, 2008; Wright, 1989; Thomson and Sacks, 2006). I will argue this equally applies to Wole Soyinka in certain respects.

Additionally, specific performative genres such as Dadaism, Surrealism, the Epic theatre, and the theatre of the Absurd have been associated with traditions in postmodernism (Potter, 1995; Guerlac, 2000; Pamatmat, 2007; Schmidt, 2005). These forms of theatre have been labeled "metatheatre" consequent to their experimentation with the narrative form, especially, the rejection of plot and the logical coherence in narration; the use of metafiction, or "historiographic metafiction" (Hutcheon, 1988); the dismissal of sequential, chronological time in favour of discontinuities; and the replacement of lifelike and overly-dissected authorial characters with ambiguous personae whose inner lives are complex, seemingly detached from authorial control and hard to explain by a simple rule of thumb (Fischer and Greiner, 2007; Feldman, 2013).

In the next section, I explore theoretically and, in some detail, the de-natured and de-centred aesthetic and thematic models presented in the postmodern drama and theatre, with a particular emphasis on what I describe as the performative techniques of postmodern theatre and the fundamentals of the sociality denoted by them.

Contours of the Postmodern Drama and Theatre

The ascription "postmodern drama and theatre" is highly contested. Whilst some theorists have seen it as emerging from the cultural and critical discourse on postmodernism in general, others have rejected the notion as too loose and imprecise (Birringer, 1991; Fuchs, 1996; Pizzato, 1998; Lehmann, 2006; Mason, 2007). For the current study, the canonical poetics and politics of postmodernism constructed by Linda Hutcheon (1988, 1989) as a concrete and discursive model of identifying the cultural and aesthetic parameters of postmodern literature are sufficient for identifying the nature of postmodern drama and theatre. As Hutcheon observes, most postmodern texts appear to excel in the use of irony, playfulness, black humour and parody to present a view of reality that is deliberately and provocatively biased, incomplete and partial. This intensely self-reflexive construction of reality is covered by Hutcheon's term "historiographic metafiction", a kind of historicism in which truth is both "falsified" as essentially the subjective account of a particular witness, and "reconstructed" as the verifiable contextual basis for a particular historical purpose. As she asserts: "To parody is not to destroy the past; in fact, to parody is both to enshrine the past and to question it" (Hutcheon, 1988:126).

Hutcheon depends on Derrida, Foucault, Barthes and Lyotard in order to construct her important politics and poetics on postmodernism. She borrowed from Derrida the technique of "deconstruction" which seeks to uncover the binaries upon which particular texts are based. Such binaries, for instance, signifier/signified; sensible/intelligible; writing/speech; passivity/activity, and so on, are opposed concepts which form a kind of double coding that needs to be separated and unpacked individually and almost autonomously in order to discover their inner meanings. From Foucault, she relies on a form of discourse analysis in which language is the important tool for investigating complex power-oriented relationships in society. Barthes' semiology furnishes her with an account of how language is "a social institution and a system of values" (Barthes, cited by Doyle and Floyd, 1973:145) subject to the creative re-rendering of the author. Writing, therefore, creates an object that can stand apart from its own author because "the text is a tissue of quotations drawn from the innumerable centers of culture," (Barthes, cited by Carano, 2008:13) rather than the individual experience or ideology of its author. It is in this sense that Barthes proclaims "the death of the author", explaining that "a text's unity lies not in its origins," or its creator, "but in its destination," or its reader or audience (Barthes, cited by Knapp, Morris and Wolf, 2011:26).

In this way, the text encompasses within its own layers innumerable levels of meaning which depend upon the reader/audience for their articulation and prioritization. This self-referential basis of the text breeds intertextuality and hyper reality and links directly to Lyotard's (1984:15) argument that postmodernism emphasises *petits récits*, or "localized" narratives, in which there is a "multiplicity of theoretical standpoints." These borrowings assist Hutcheon to found a poetics of postmodern literature on the parodical properties of language in which the notions of self-referentiality, self-reflexivity, intertextuality, pastiche, temporal distortion, maximalism, minimalism, fabulation, poioumena, paranoia, magic realism and technoculture become important parameters. As Hutcheon notes:

> In challenging the seamless quality of the history/fiction (or world/art) join implied by realist narrative, postmodern fiction does not disconnect itself from history or the world. It foregrounds and thus contests the conventionality and unacknowledged ideology of that assumption of seamlessness and asks its readers to question the process by which we represent ourselves and our world to ourselves and to become aware of the means by which we *make* sense of and *construct* order out of experience in our particular culture. We cannot avoid representation. We *can* try to avoid fixing our notion of it and assuming it to be transhistorical and transcultural. We can also study how representation legitimizes and privileges certain kinds of knowledge including certain kinds of historical knowledge. (Hutcheon, 1988:23)

The consequence of all of this is what Hutcheon characterises as "historiographic metafiction":

> Through a double process of installing and ironizing, parody signals how present representations come from past ones and what ideological consequences derive from both continuity and difference. (Hutcheon, 1989:93)

Accordingly, Hutcheon remarks that "postmodernism is a contradictory phenomenon, one that uses and abuses, installs and then subverts the very concepts it challenges" (Hutcheon, 1988:3). Through parody the postmodern text becomes a tool for critiquing a number of thematic and aesthetic assumptions: 1) (a la Barthes) the authorial originality and the givenness of the author's proprietary role in the possible meanings of the text; 2) (a la Derrida) reality as a linear, lineal and self-autonomous social construct; 3) (a la Foucault) the governmentality in which the capitalist principles of ownership and commoditisation determine the creation and consumption (mass access, critical reception, modes of reading or performance, etc.) of the text; 4) (a la Lyotard) the multiple standpoints of meaning or identity which subvert the temporal naturalness of the text, de-naturalising it and elevating its artificiality; 5) history as an objective approach to truth (this is turned on its head through pastiche and fabulation into metahistory); 6) the possible apolitical and ahistorical status of the text (this is denied and, through maximalism and minimalism, there is an incipient argument against the notion of a neutral or non-ideological text); and, finally, 7) the autonomy of the text and its creator as the regulators of meaning, separate from either a mass audience/readership, re-performances, etc..

Hutcheon's thesis of postmodern poetics has been challenged, for instance by Stephen Baker (2000a; 2000b), as limited to an exclusive literary genre denoted by "historiographic metafiction" to the exclusion of other postmodern forms (Baker, 2000a:5). I do not think this is the case, and Baker is reading Hutcheon rather narrowly. However, whilst I accept the appropriateness of Hutcheon's model, including her semantic treatment of the notion of postmodernity *contra* postmodernism, both in her politics and poetics of postmodernism she fails to acknowledge the liminoid characteristics of the postmodern era and the postmodern condition which, in my view, actually, both culturally and historically are the very templates of postmodernity and postmodernism (d'Haen, Bertens, and Bertens, 1994; Taylor and Winquist, 2003). It is the case that the universal liminality heralded by the Second World War and its conclusion in 1945 (Szakolczai, 2003; Broadhurst, 1999) is the continuing foreground of postmodernism, and I would argue that where the theatrical space is dominated by liminality, the consequences will include the fragmentation of time and reality, unpredictability of character and action, and the uncontrolled chaos and artificiality which are the constant elements and methods of postmodern drama and theatre. Other important nodes of history, such as imperialism and postcolonialism, are decisive tributaries of the liminality of the postmodern condition (Bhabha, 2012).

In short, since 1945, beginning in Europe and the US, a paradigm shift occurred both historically and culturally, in which the pre-Second World War sense of modernity – human progress as a unilinear concept, society as a nearly homogenous script of the governing and labouring classes, and international relations as a set of self-apparent consensual principles – ruptured completely into liminal and liminoid categories. In my second mini book, **Modernism and Liminality** (Ilori, 2014), I described these categories as, principally, my borrowings from van Gennep (1977) and Victor Turner (1969).

Historically and culturally, liminal periods take on different poses: hierarchical structures are dissolved or temporarily suspended; established traditions are contested; the cause-effect logic of natural history is disrupted, and the future is no longer something anticipated or predictable but is webbed into a fluid but complex, contradictory and permeable structure of rationality (Turner, 1957, 1982). Society becomes liminoid in that all aspects of received wisdom fall under intense scrutiny, and existing rules of thought, self-understanding, and behaviour are unscrewed, melted down and discarded as the very structure of society itself is shaken loose or temporarily suspended, in search of potential alternatives (Turner, 1987; Turnbull, 1990). By implication, the phenomenon represented by the Second World War and other nodal historical events ruptured the "normative structure" of the world (as known) and led to an "anti-structure" containing potential alternatives. To borrow Brian Sutton-Smith's (1972) description of liminal and liminoid categories:

> The normative structure represents the working equilibrium, the anti-structure represents the latent system of potential alternatives from which novelty will arise when contingencies in the normative system require it. We might more correctly call this second system the proto-structural system because it is the precursor of innovative normative forms. It is the source of new culture. (Sutton-Smith, 1972: 18-19)

In my view, this accounts also for the performative techniques of postmodern theatre and the fundamentals of the sociality denoted by them. Borrowing from the experimental theatre techniques from Constantin Stanislavsky to Peter Brook (Roose-Evans, 1970; Yordon, 1997), and the seminal (even avant-gardist) approaches to drama from Samuel Beckett to Wole Soyinka, I would cite the following as apical characteristics of postmodern theatre and drama:

1. There is a self-conscious experimental approach to play production, determined to challenge and subvert the traditional notions of reality as an organic metaphor for a singular, unproblematic worldview (Best and Kellner, 1997);

2. The influence of several types of art and media forms to create a production with a pastiche-feel, and a kind of intertextuality reflecting the heterogeneity of cultural forms in

real practice, without regard for the artificial division of culture into "highbrow" and popular forms comes across patently (Lyotard, 1984; Jameson, 1991; Nicol, 2009);

3. Plot, action and character are fragmented, paradoxical and imagistic to give the audience innumerable codes and handles for plotting the play according to their own preferences (Artaud, 2010; Frank and Tamborino, 2000; Brown, 2001)

4. The traditional assemblage of acts and scenes are re-arranged into a multiplicity of dramatic moments and become vistas for perceiving the different, sometimes, contradictory, inner meanings of the production by the audience (Michelfelder and Palmer, 1989; Gallagher, 2002);

5. Re-performances are methodically imbued with some new "gestalt" (a new shape, a new figuring, etc.) so that each production results in a unique spectacle (Schmid and Kesteren, 1984; Alter, 1990; Meyer-Dinkgräfe, 2005)

6. From rehearsals to opening night, the production is constructed around what might be termed an improvisatory translation of the text, or thematic directions in which all the production crew participates through their own unique contribution (Johnstone, 2012; Smith

and Dean, 1997; Peters 2009; Hoffmann, 2005);

7. The reality that the production eventually presents is a montage, a simulacrum or ironic mock-up, deliberately constructed as a critique or shadow of something or someone in real life (Gabriel and Ilcan, 2004; Malkin, 1999).

I admit that these are techniques of production which may or may not be seeded into the text by the playwright but will remain underlying inferences in the architecture of the text.

Moreover, in consequence of postmodernism and, especially, the liminality that I have argued as its important envelope, I will argue that the fundamentals of the sociality denoted in the postmodern play will revolve around three key nominative categories, namely, abjection, alterity and abstraction. I use the word "abjection" in a poststructuralist sense: the grammar of a postmodern play, its operative cultural register will inherently include aspects which upset the consensus that underpins a particular social order and the conventional processes of cultural identity. Here, I am adopting and extending the use of "abjection" by Julia Kristeva (1982) for whom the notion of the abject is that which, as a Subject or Object, is rejected by or disturbed by a certain cognition of offence, the transgression of some established consensus or social norm. The Subject-Object distinctions in a real historical but temporal space are important, but they are permeable and help to shape the interactions within a given space (Alway, 1995; Hillman, 1999).

Such interactions determine the prevailing atmosphere of both the performance space and the social space, and may convey a palpable sense of liminality where the dialectics, as we find in temporal and ritual scenarios, involve movements between various normative categories. Accordingly, it is not unlikely that the social processes, the forms of morality, rationality and authority extant within the space will be subjected at various points to different levels of deliberate assaults both as a method of identity-formation as well as identity-destruction or damage.

The processes of reflection, accounting for differences, absorption, tolerance, etc. can then lead to manifold symbolic discontinuities in Subject-Object interactions (Oliver, 1993; Smith, 1998). The discontinuities can include instances or states of abjection, when a person's act, or even language, silence, stillness or gest, violates the spatial and social relationship between Subject and Object in a way that breaks the protective boundaries of cultural or social acceptances, and inaugurates various patterns of pain, horror, alienation, etc. which seek to destroy or deface the cultural identity and integrity of the Subject or Object. What results is a sort of cognitive dissonance (Festinger, 1962), in which the holistic relationship between Subject and Object breaks down and is overtaken by disequilibrium, and an overtly conflictual atmosphere of undesirable neuroses, such as dirt, disease, defeat, deprivation, dismay, culpability, resentment, discomfiture, and disquiet, amongst others.

Consequently, the liminal space transmutes into a place of abjection, a place where "abjected" things, values, ideas, or beings inhabit and a somewhat amoral universe prevails.

This whole process includes a certain tendency towards "Otherness" (**Lévinas, 1991**) by the personae within the play, and this permeates the overall anti-structural and antifoundational ambience of the interactions between them as Subject and Object, as Subject-Object (a condition in which **man is both knowing subject and the object of his own study**" – Foucault, cited by Oksala (2005:57)) and the symbolic or temporal space that they occupy. There is alterity, the opportunity and facility to construct a shadow or shadows of Self in contrast and negation of the proximate identities of Others as an imbrication of the processes which create a series of "cultural others" and consign them to that domain of thought, discourse or praxis in which they are represented as exotic, imagistic, marginal, peripheral, incidental, imaginary, originary, dangerous, disposable, dispensable, etc.

This in itself is a kind of abstraction which reduces the ample reality and historical significance of the "Other" to a handy category of cultural experience in order to satisfy the conditions and parameters of the Subject exclusively. The phenomenology of the Other is stripped out and replaced by a hollow transcendence in which the very Being of the Other is distanced from its actuality and treated, not as a concrete, physical and objective persona or thing, but as an imagined idea, a constructed concept, a simulacrum, an image that can be flexibly deployed to meet the requirements of the Subject.

I suggest that abjection, alterity and abstraction are principal taxonomic categories for exploring and explaining postmodernist sensibilities both in society and across diverse cultural forms. I suggest that these taxonomic elements within the liminal space are the fundamentals of the sociality we encounter in postmodern drama and theatre. In the next section, I aim to uncover these fundamentals and the performative practices they entail in Soyinka's **A Play of Giants** and **The Beatification of Area Boy.**

Postmodern Performative Practices and Sociality
"A Play of Giants" **and** "The Beatification of Area Boy"

Giants and **Beatification** are completely plotless and exist as shards of narratives on an endless plateau of concerns and grievances against extant forms of political and moral rationality and authority. In his notes to **Giants**, Soyinka discloses that the "form" of **Giants** was borrowed from Jean Genet's "The Balcony" but the slight relationship between **Giants** and **Balcony** consists supremely of the excessive focus on the creation and (ab)use of political power through various forms of violation of a prevailing social order and how this is theatricised in grotesque parody in both plays. **Giants** is built around the grotesqueries of Kamini, Touboum, Kasco and Gunema (African Heads of State) in Kamini's Bugaran embassy in front of the United Nations complex in Manhattan, New York.

The parodic theatricality of **Giants** lampoons these antiheroes as historical references to the presidents of Uganda (Idi Amin), the Democratic Republic of Congo (Mobutu Sese Seko), Central African Republic (Jean-Baptiste Bokassa) and Equatorial Guinea (Macias Nguema). They had gathered to attend a session of the United Nations but were also responding to a request for a cultural work of art representative of their country to be displayed in a lobby of the U.N. as a kind of mood music for the occasion. Kamini enlarged the request into a full-fledged collective bust of himself and the others, and as play opens, three of them, to be joined by the fourth, were sitting in front of a White sculptor from Madame Tussauds in London. The rest of the play is their collective reflexivity on the mystique of political power, its majesty and meanness.

We are aware of the abjection, alterity and abstraction that characterise their personal acts and introspection but they remain distanced from the oddity and its odious scale, bridged as it were by similar propensities in those who assist them to manage the machinery and mania of power – principally, ex-colonial powers and the superpowers (the USA and the USSR) – and local props, ranging from petrified administration and security personnel to foreign journalists and intellectual and cultural apologists. The session at the U.N. never happened, the bust was an unfinished work, and the play closes with Kamini holding all his embassy guests (including the other presidents, Russian and American diplomats and the Secretary-General of the U.N.) as hostages, and directing a violent assault at the U.N.

complex across the street because he had been overthrown back in Bugara and, in his paranoia, this could only have succeeded with the help of the U.N. The entire farce freezes upon the hostages' "horror-stricken faces in various postures." But "the Sculptor works on in slow motion. Slow fade." (**Giants**, 82)

Beatification is also a grand theatrical spectacle, a vast expanse of a dreamy, nightmarish world in which everything is chaotic, unpredictable, zany and preposterous. In 82 pages, at least **Giants** was organised into two parts; contrastively, **Beatification** runs into 100 pages, has no formal parts, no division into acts or scenes but gushes on like an endless meandering gurgling stream, packed with society's sewage from top to bottom. The people in **Beatification** are vagrants, petty traders, petty barbers, petty shoppers, petty thieves, and the emerging middle class (big shoppers, big bosses, etc.) linked in seamy acts with the established acquisitive political class.

However, through parody, at various points in **Beatification**, they all belong to one social class – the rubbish of society, except that in dark solecisms, tongue-in-cheek camaraderie and witty aphorisms, **Beatification's** petty people sometimes achieve pretensions to a form of nobility that is not theirs by any substantial moral virtue. Sanda, a university drop-out, is the Area Boy, or the head of the "area" – a metonym for the backwoods shopping suburb and ragged residences in rundown Lagos. He is a self-employed Security Guard in control of a number of petty criminals. They and the urbane Lagosians who cut across their turf occasionally have different forms of power – cultic power (charmers and diviners), turf power (Sanda and his retinue), money power (noveau-riche, middle class Lagosians), and political power (the military and their top civil administrators).

Consequently, **Beatification** is filled with disconcerting narratives on the principles of power, the practices of power, and the people in power and those under someone's power as they struggle to shape their own dreams in response to the chaos and corruption bedevilling their society. The play closes with the acts of Sanda and his retinue inconceivably concluding in a lavish wedding rite, organised by the political class for one of their own but upended when the bride chose Sanda instead of finalising her nuptial procedure with the assumed bridegroom. This *mise en abîme* that marks the end of **Beatification** parallels its gross artificiality and underlines the anti-structural and antifoundational register of the cultural paradigm that is its social world.

Essentially, both **Giants** and **Beatification** lack logical coherence in narration as sequential and chronological time is displaced by a conversational rhythm that jumps from place to place – from quasi-historical collective reminiscences to exaggerated personal vignettes; from the quotidian ebb and flow of routinised social acts to the surreal cosmos of international politics and diplomacy; from epigrammatic references to political violence and the violation of social rights to embarrassing shenanigans of everyone (including nations) driven by self-interest and opportunism. There is altogether a piquant amoral universe in which the fragmentation of time and reality, the unpredictability of character and action, and the uncontrolled chaos and artificiality of the social world in both plays serve to parallel the discontinuities in the narratives and the ambiguities of the anti-heroes. Aesthetically and thematically, reality and rationality, authority and morality, structure and agency are de-natured and de-centred through irony, playfulness, and black humour. Everyone's version of social truth is deliberately and provocatively grotesque, subversive, controversial and fractional. History becomes a self-reflexive construction of reality, the subjective account of a particular witness which is "reconstructed" as the contextual background for some self-serving national or personal purpose.

Examples abound.

In **Giants**, Gunema provides several chilling accounts of the voodoo-basis of his hold on power and his rationality is comprehensive: "When politics has become routine, organised, we who are gifted naturally with leadership, after a while, we cease to govern, to lead: we exist I think, in a rare space which is – power." (**Giants** 12) Elsewhere, he asserts: "Some people are born to power. Others are – cattle. They need ring in their nose for us to lead." (**Giants** 21) As a result his authority over his subjects is exclusive: "When I look at each one of my ministers, or army officer, he knows I am looking into the heart, into the very soul of his village. He know that I see through his head into the head of his wife, his children, his father and mother and grandfather and uncles and all his dependents, all his kith and kin, living or dead… yes, including the dead ones. It is he who must choose whether they lie in peace in their graves because, *la culpabilidad* the - er – guilt, it extends beyond the grave." (**Giants** 27) Such mystique is reinforced by sexual violation of his subjects in which power becomes a form of elixir, an aphrodisiac, obtained by violating the victim's spouse (**Giants** 69-70).

The majesty (or vainglory) of power is picked up by Touboum for whom the wanton carnage perpetrated by his forces, assisted by ex-colonial forces, in pursuit of armed rebels was a proud accomplishment (**Giants** 28-30). Kasco's majesty is different. He is a self-proclaimed Emperor, above and beyond politics: "power comes only with the death of politics. That is why I choose to become emperor. I place myself beyond politics. At the moment of coronation, I signal to the world that I transcend the intrigues and mundaneness of politics. Now I inhabit only the pure realm of power." (**Giants** 31). Kamini tops them all. He proudly compares himself to Hitler (**Giants** 22) and provides instances of despicable brutality, inhumanity and bestiality – his gross abuse of power re-defines the meanness of power.

The intense self-reflexive acts and disclosures of these political freaks are juxtaposed with the condescension, cooperation and cringing loyalty of several functionaries and ex-colonial powers. They sustain the machinery and mania of power and become victims of the irrationality and delusion of Kamini. Indeed, paranoia becomes the main referent for the actions of everyone in **Giants** – it is the amoral switch that Kamini and the other presidents use to deflect attention from their abuses; it is the authority behind the interferences of ex-colonial powers in the affairs of their ex-colonies; and the rationality for the obsequious conduct of state functionaries, the foreign press and cultural/ideological apologists for Kamini and others. The eclectic narrative strands are bolstered by the jaunty shifts between historical personages (such as Napoleon, de Gaulle, Papa Doc, Hitler, Dag Hammarskjöld and Chaka) and the events surrounding them to pure fabulation enacted to exaggerate the buffoonery and bestiality of the anti-heroes.

The narratives are dramatic moments and obvious markers of mise-en-scène which give the unfolding events a pastiche-feel. Additionally, appurtenances, such as the flushing toilet, sirens, police cars screeching, machine-gunners, rocket launchers, exploding grenades, etc. present some sort of technoculture which heightens the theatrical "gestalt" in **Giants**, bestowing a firm sense of contrivance and artificiality. Similar examples are multiply instantiated in **Beatification**.

There is an endless array of characters in **Beatification**, each one the latest trope on the extended theatricality of the pun on the principles (ethics) of power, the practices of power and the people of power and under power. Ethically, power is rooted in the norms of self-aggrandisement, self-interest, and self-ingratiation. As a result, power is practised abusively, wantonly, and derogatorily. Powerful people get rich at the expense of others, most are members of the military and political class whose wealth is based on fraudulent appropriation of state funds; others secure their wealth through the criminal underworld, or mysterious murders for harvesting body parts for money-making rituals and effigies; others mingle amongst the thronging masses on foot or on public transport to spirit away people's genitalia for money-making rituals.

These are the powerful people in **Beatification**, and they control the destiny of others through patronage, paternalism, fear, fraud and cultic influence. People under the tyranny of power live in the shadows of society and accommodate themselves to the noise and nuisance of everyday life. The routes to power are listed by Sanda: "Cocaine. 419 swindles. Godfathering or mothering armed robbers. Or after a career with the police. Or the Army, if you're lucky to grab a political post. Then you retire at forty – as a General who has never fought a war. Or you start your own church, or mosque. That's getting more and more popular." (**Beatification 240**)

In numerous songs and spectacle, the underbelly of society is turned up as seamy, superstitious and sensational (**Beatification 243-245, 251-259, 291-296, 303-313, 316-326**). Each character provides their own unique commentary on the ills of state and the downhill direction of their society. The commentaries are multifocal, conveying contradictory and controversial standpoints in the culture and history of Lagos and the country. **Beatification** rumbles on from one exposé to the next, packing up increasingly grisly and gnomic references to historical events such as the Nigerian Civil War, the profound wastage of oil earnings, disastrous international events (the invasion of Iraq, and Hitler's "Final Solution", for instance), government statements and economic policies (for instance, the Udoji Award of inflated salaries to public servants), the slum clearance in Maroko, etc.

Entirely, all elements of corruption are covered in song, scenery and spectacle and **Beatification** is weighed down in the end by a surfeit of pastiche, paranoia, and techniques for inducing audience participation (for instance, popular lyrics, mass demonstrations, mass media reports, Afro "high life" entertainers, popular stories of vanishing genitals, abduction of albinos and mob justice). Moreover, the "broad sliding doors of tinted glass" into the shopping plaza, fronted by the open slummy market that Sanda inhabits, is deployed to great effect as a form of technoculture which reflects and distorts "traffic scenes from the main street". In fact, stage directions insist that "When the doors slide open, the well-stocked interior of consumer items – a three-dimensional projection or photo blow-up will suffice – contrast vividly with the slummy exterior". (**Beatification 231**)

As a result of the multiple uses of technoculture and localised narratives in **Giants** and **Beatification** and the parodic assets of language, action, setting and characterisation, there is a grossly "simulated" version of reality – a profoundly distorted copy which affects us in its own right as a model of truth, even in its hyperreality. The world of both plays is a constant reaction to and rejection of a social structure that is dehumanising and the subhuman cultural and political governmentality (a la Foucault) which is its prevailing method of discourse, morality, authority and rationality.

In its holism, the structure of society that we encounter in **Giants** and **Beatification** significantly diminishes the capacity of individual agents to substantially reformulate their world. In spite of this or even as a consequence, as agents, the people in both plays occupy a liminal space in which their social interactions are ironically overwhelmingly anti-structural, and the fundamentals of the sociality denoted in their experiences include abjection, alterity and abstraction. In both plays, through parody and irony, the operative cultural register is a vicious critique of the social order and conventional cultural and political processes which allow Kamini, Touboum, Kasco, and Gunema (**Giants**) and the Area Boy and his retinue, and the corrupt military and civilian functionaries (**Beatification**) the huge space for their violations. Their narratives are charged with odious details, which are so frequently graphic and quite disturbing as examples of corruption, sadism and masochism.

In the liminal space construed by both plays, cultural identity and morality, authority and rationality are undermined by the repellent nature of the philosophy and social acts of all the characters in **Giants** (except the Sculptor), and many of the characters in **Beatification**, at different levels of subtlety. The overweening intensities of chaos, indeterminacy and randomness in both plays establish a cultural environment in which manifold symbolic discontinuities are ritualised both as familiar and foreign properties of the social space. Through shades of irony and black humour, the Subjects criticize their own acts as they transmute from Subject to Object, or simply as a Subject-Object category. Accordingly, the cognitive dissonance we experience in both plays is largely informed by the overtly coded conflictual values in the acts of the various personae and the resultant environment of paranoia, guilt, filth, discomfiture and disquiet, amongst others. Consequently, in **Giants** and **Beatification**, social space echoes with abjection and is occupied by a series of abjected beings, values and ideas.

Furthermore, abjection is strongly complemented by alterity in both plays. To deflect blame from them, people in **Giants** and **Beatification** construct a view of themselves as Subject and of others as Object. There then ensues a nearly circular argument of justifying the unjustifiable by a relentless tendency towards "Otherness". Blame, guilt, perfidy, and other moral constructs are then spread around as Subjects become Objects, and Objects become Subjects, and even in Subject-Object categories of self-reflexivity and self-representation. This is displayed blatantly in **Giants** and becomes its substantial caricature of colonialism, postcolonialism, and superpower complicity in global political instability, violence and venality.

Although subtler in **Beatification**, alterity grants the Area Boy and his retinue the *raisons d'être* to construct their shadowy existence and petty criminal underworld as a valid norm in contrast to and negation of the proximate identities of the military and political class whose sway of power over their lives is condemnable and objectionable. But alterity is a two-way traffic: in the eyes of the apparatus of government, Sanda and his community are "Others" who must be consigned to a social realm in which no-one is above the law and the "rule of law" for once can be asserted aggressively to their detriment. In other words, in **Giants** and **Beatification**, "Subject" and "Object" categories demonstrate the processes which create a series of "cultural others" and represent them according to the requirements of the Subject.

Principally, as we discover in **Giants** and **Beatification**, "cultural others" are guilty, inferior, pathetic, vulgar, disposable and dispensable. Of course, "cultural others" are an abstraction, they are the imagistic construction of the Subject. Their ample reality and historical significance have been hollowed out and their being as a social phenomenon has been reduced to a handy category of cultural experience to satisfy the conditions and criticisms of the Subject exclusively. Consequently, there is an underlying discourse in **Giants** and **Beatification** in which, for aesthetic effect, thematic sanguinity and ideological respectability, everyone is tainted and almost unredeemable, and overly satirised and caricaturised.

Giants skewers everyone and every institution it encompasses, but dramatises postcolonialism as an unnatural disorder, implicated largely by the (sub)mentality of the ruling authorities in ex-colonies and the continuing mischief of ex-colonial powers and opportunistic superpower political machinations. The postcolonial discourse in **Giants** may be a fierce criticism of the levers of political and economic control inside and outside ex-colonies, but it is ultimately empty of any transformative power or vision. In a slightly more genteel fashion, **Beatification** represents postcoloniality as the conditionality within culture and the political and economic system which inherently breeds social aberrations and limits the scope ominously for eventual remedial action. There are ironic moments when **Beatification** appears sympathetic to the pain and penury of the powerless and the voiceless, but it soon defaults to its main aim and parodies their puerility, naivety and incredulity. In the end, the postcolonial discourse in **Beatification** is overly pessimistic and despairing and merely squints at any favourable future prospects.

The Fourth Stage – Authoricide and Artifice

So far, I have treated these two plays without any direct reference to Soyinka's authorial cultural and political interests in the unfolding of the disparate events dramatised in **Giants** and **Beatification**. This is deliberate: firstly, I subscribe to the Barthian disclosure that the author dies where the text begins; secondly, the thematic and aesthetic "formularies" that I have noted in **Giants** and **Beatification** are actually heavy stage props with clear authoricidal propensities. As pieces of artifice, they allow us to bypass the author's proprietary role in the possible meanings of the text and attack any concept of reality or history as a linear, lineal and self-autonomous social construct. The multiplicity of characters morphing, altering and disappearing only to re-appear in other guises and for endless theatrical and thematic necessities presents access to several standpoints of meaning, and cultural and social identities in a manner that subverts the temporal naturalness of the text, de-naturalising it and elevating its artificiality.

Giants and **Beatification**, through pastiche and fabulation, conflate facts and fiction, history and metahistory, achieving the implausible and logically impossible effect of a truthful, serious and yet sensational and overblown portrayal of historicised personages and specious factual narratives. On the surface, this kind of approach to historicity is confusedly porous, apolitical and ahistorical. However, its aesthetic and ideological ramifications suggest that actually the whole is greater than the sum of its parts - **Giants** and **Beatification** are left-of-centre guerrilla pieces of theatre launched against decadent right wing values and social and cultural practices. Through maximalism, mainly, both plays present a clear, even if sometimes inchoate, ideological argument framing the postcolonial state and its functionaries as abject beings, international powers as supercilious and exploitative, and ordinary people as mired in a self-authored culture of abject naivety, puerility, and materialism.

Everything in both plays appears left to chance due to the self-conscious and experimental approach to characterisation, action and setting. If there is anything organic in the presentation that we encounter, it is the world of mayhem, madness and mythic metaphors in which a system of meanings and an apparent culture of symbolic mediation of history subsists. Otherwise, everything is jaunty, improvisational, disordered and spontaneous. The appurtenances of art and media forms give both plays additional performative ambience which increases the pastiche-feel, and a certain intertextuality imitating the heterogeneity of cultural forms in society and how "highbrow" and popular strands of culture co-mingle in everyday life.

In **Giants** and **Beatification**, the narrative flow is constantly disrupted and replete with discontinuities and fragmentary information; action and character are mainly asynchronous, paradoxical and imagistic to give the reader/audience innumerable codes and handles for "plotting" the play according to their own preferences. The plays are ingested with audience-participatory tools, especially, as the traditional assemblage of acts and scenes are simply a series of dramatic moments and vistas for perceiving the different, sometimes, contradictory, inner meanings of the plays by the audience. This ensures a discernible trace of "gestalt" – modes of perception and cognition – that actors, directors and audiences can use to mine the meanings layered into the text of both plays and prioritise them according to their own preferences. In this way, Soyinka's effacement is complete in the montage and ironic mock-up of fact and fiction in **Giants** and **Beatification**, and in their obvious postmodern turn, the playwright's vision is part of the liminoid properties of the text.

Conclusion – The (At)Traction of Transhistorical Paradigms

My central argument is that postmodernism is a continuing cultural category both as a matter of history and theory. Although patently a Eurocentric construct, its transhistorical character enables it to have referents in cultures well outside of Europe as purely materialist dialectics in which the conjunctions of imperialism, capitalism and postcolonialism – as a minimum condition - have elevated both neo-Enlightenment and contra-Enlightenment concerns as global cultural and theoretical forms of discourse in different modes of production of knowledge. The polemics of the emergence, nature and duration of the postmodern turn will, arguably, continue far into the 21st century despite the announcement of its extinction by several theorists, including Alan Kirby (2007) and Raoul Eshelman (2009) for whom the hallmarks of postmodernism – pastiche, parody and parataxis – have become less endemic in post-postmodern literature and the arts.

However, as I have pointed out, the new labels that have emerged to describe the alternatives to postmodernism or postmodernity, for instance, Bourriaud's "altermodern"; Lipovetsky's and Charles' "hypermodernity"; Eshelman's "performatism"; Samuels' "automodernity"; and Kirby's "digimodernism" do not, essentially, reflect a break with postmodernism but represent a continuum in which culture is constantly a movement towards something yet undefinable but still within the postmodern environment. Although these new forms of cognition and discourse are being incubated within postmodernism, they also tend to be reactions to it, and seem to be affirming, not a return to modernism, or a conclusive break with postmodernism, but vacillation between both cultural references.

As a result, for their signification, they still depend largely on the theoretical discourses advanced by Foucault, Derrida, Lyotard and Baudrillard and so far, probably, are best articulated in the propositions of Timotheus

Vermeulen and Robin van den Akker (2010) who have characterised this new signification as "metamodernism". This, in my view, suggests that metamodernism is not something that *follows after* but *flows from* postmodernism, and I will pick this up in more detail when I examine aspects of metamodernism in the theatre of Wole Soyinka.

Finally, arguably, based on the liminal criteria in the culture dramatised in Soyinka's theatre, the different versions of postcoloniality traceable in the entire corpus, and the engaging craft which is the vehicle for his thematic and aesthetic concerns, postmodernism becomes a transhistorical cultural paradigm which ventilates the controversial and seamy politics of Soyinka's "people". As **Giants** and **Beatification** demonstrate, this is a paradigm that shifts continuously even within particular texts and articulates a subjective view of history in which the elements of structure and agency are often in chaotic tension, unpredictable and open-ended. Perhaps, this explains the complexities and bewildering array of metaphors and motifs in Soyinka's dramaturgy. If, as Barthes argues, the author dies where the text begins, the freedom to examine each play in the corpus in terms of its own people and their culture, and the performative practices and the forms of discourse behind them as modes of cultural production and exchange, provides the latitude we require for a deconstructive approach to Soyinka's theatre. In this instance, postmodernism as a form of heuristic historicism has helped to decomplexify Soyinka, providing a discursive schema for interrogating his plays as cultural artifacts.

Select Bibliography and References

Acheraïou, A. (2008). Rethinking Postcolonialism: Colonialist Discourse in Modern Literatures and the Legacy of Classical Writers. London: Palgrave Macmillan.

Adas, M. (1989). Machines as the Measure of Men: Science, Technology, and Ideologies of Western Dominance. Ithaca: Cornell University Press.

Alter, J. (1990). A Sociosemiotic Theory of Theatre. Pennsylvania: University of Pennsylvania Press.

Alway, J. (1995). Critical Theory and Political Possibilities. New York: Greenwood Publishing Group.

Anderson, C. (2012). Subaltern Lives: Biographies of Colonialism in the Indian Ocean World, 1790-1920. Cambridge: Cambridge University Press.

Appiah, K.A. (1991). Is the Post- in Postmodernism the Post- in Postcolonial? In Critical Inquiry. Vol. 17. No. 2 (Winter, 1991). pp. 336-357

Artaud, A. (2010). The Theatre and Its double. London: One World Classics.

Assiter, A. (1984). "Althusser and Structuralism". The British Journal of Sociology. Vol. 35, no. 2, Oxford: Blackwell Publishing, pp. 272–296.

Baker, S. (2000). The Fiction of Postmodernity. London: Rowman & Littlefield.

Ballantyne, T. (2012). Webs of Empire: Locating New Zealand's Colonial Past. London: Bridget Williams.

Banham, G. (2003). Kant's Practical Philosophy: From Critique to Doctrine. London: Palgrave Macmillan.

Banham, G. (2006). Kant's Transcendental Imagination. London: Palgrave Macmillan.

Barbeito, M. (ed.) (2000) Modernity, Modernism, Postmodernism. Santiago: Universidade de Santiago de Compostela.

Barker, F., Hulme, P. and Iverson, M. (1994). Colonial Discourse/Postcolonial Theory. Manchester: Manchester University Press.

Barthes, R. (1977). Image, Music, Text. (Trans.) Stephen Heath. London: Fontana Press.

Barthes, R. (1998). "The Death of the Author". Art and Interpretation: An Anthology of Readings in Aesthetics and the Philosophy of Art. (ed.) Eric Dayton (1998). Peterborough, Ont.: Broadview. (pp. 383-386).

Baudrillard, J. (1983). Simulations. Manchester: MIT Press.

Baudrillard, J. (1991). Seduction. London: St. Martin's Press.

Baudrillard, J. (1994). Simulacra and Simulation. (Trans.) Sheila Faria Glaser. Michigan: Michigan University Press.

Baudrillard, J. (2005). The Sytem of Objects. London: Verso Books.

Benhabib, S. (1995). "Feminism and Postmodernism". In Benhabib, S. (ed.) (1995). Feminist Contentions: A Philosophical Exchange. London: Routledge. (pp. 17-34)

Bereano, P. (1977). Technology as a Social and Political Phenomenon. New York: Wiley & Sons.

Bertens, H. (2004). The Idea of the Postmodern: A History. London: Routledge.

Bertens, H. and Natoli, J. (eds.) (2002). Postmodernism: The Key Figures. Oxford: Blackwell.

Best, S. and Kellner, D. (1997). The Postmodern Turn. New York: The Guildford Press.

Bhabha, H.K. (1994, 2012). The Location of Culture. Oxon: Routledge.

Bhabha, H.K. (2011). Our Neighbours, Ourselves: Contemporary Reflections on Survival. Berlin/New York: Walter de Gruyter.

Bhabha, H.K. (ed.) (1990, 2013). Nation and Narration. Oxon: Routledge.

Birringer, J.H. (1991). Theatre, Theory, Postmodernism. Indiana: Indiana University Press.

Blanken, L. (2012). Rational Empires: Institutional Incentives and Imperial Expansion. Chicago: University Of Chicago Press.

Bogue, R. (2002) "Gilles Deleuze and Felix Guattari". In Postmodernism: The Key Figures. (eds.) Bertens, H. and Natoli, J. Oxford: Blackwell.

Bourriaud, N. (2009). Altermodern: Tate Triennial 2009. London: Tate Publishing.

Bradshaw, D. and Dettmar, K.J.H. (eds.) (2008). A Companion to Modernist Literature and Culture. Oxford: Blackwell Publishing.

Bricmont, J. (1998). Intellectual Impostures. London: Profile Books.

Broadhurst, S. (1999). Liminal Acts: A Critical Overview of Contemporary Performance and Theory. London: Continuum.

Brook, P. (1968) The Empty Space. New York: Touchstone.

Brown, W. (2001). Politics Out of History. Princeton: Princeton University Press.

Burkitt, K. (2012). Literary Form As Postcolonial Critique: Epic Proportions. Farnham: Ashgate Publishing.

Burton, A. (ed.) (2003) After the Imperial Turn: Thinking with and Through the Nation. Durham, N.C.: Duke University Press.

Butler, J. (1995). "Contingent Foundations". In Benhabib, S. (ed.) (1995). Feminist Contentions: A Philosophical Exchange. London: Routledge. (pp. 35-58)

Callinicos, A. (1990) Against Post Modernism: A Marxist Critique. London: St. martin's Press.

Callinicos, A. (2006). The Resources of Critique. Cambridge: Polity Press.

Castells, M. (1997). The Power of Identity, The Information Age: Economy, Society and Culture Vol. II. Oxford: Blackwell.

Castells, M. (2009). The Rise of the Network Society. Oxford: Wiley-Blackwell.

Caughie, P.L. (1991). Virginia Woolf & Postmodernism: Literature in Quest & Question of Itself. Illinois: University of Illinois Press.

Chakrabarty, D. (1992). "Postcoloniality and the Artifice of History: Who Speaks for "Indian" Pasts?" Representations, No. 37, Special Issue: Imperial Fantasies and Postcolonial Histories. (Winter, 1992), pp. 1-26.

Chomsky, N. (2004). Language and Politics. Edinburgh: A.K. Press.

Chomsky, N. (2006). Language and Mind. Cambridge: Cambridge University Press.

Chomsky, N. (2008). Interventions. London: Penguin Books.

Conteh-Morgan, J. and Olaniyan, T. (eds.) (2004). African Drama and Performance. Indiana: Indiana University Press.

Cornel, W. (1993). Prophetic Thought in Postmodern Times (Beyond Eurocentrism and Multiculturalism. (Vol. 1) Monroe, Maine: Common Courage Press.

Crosthwaite, P. (2009). Trauma, Postmodernism and the Aftermath of World War II Basingstoke: Palgrave Macmillan.

D'Haen, T., and Bertens, H. (1994). Liminal Postmodernisms: The Postmodern, the (Post-) Colonial, and the (Post-) Feminist. Atlanta, G.A.: Rodopi.

Daunton, M. and Rieger, B. (2001). Meanings of Modernity: Britain from the Late-Victorian Era to World War II. Oxford: Berg Publishers.

Deleuze, G. (2002). "How Do We Recognise Structuralism?" In Desert Islands and Other Texts 1953-1974. (Trans.) David Lapoujade. (ed.) Michael Taormina. Los Angeles and New York: Semiotext(e) pp. 170–192.

Deleuze, G. and Guattari, F. (1994). What Is Philosophy? (Trans.) Graham Burchell and Hugh Tomlinson. London: Verso.

Delueze, G. (2005). Difference and Repetition. London: Continuum.

Derrida, J. (1976). Of Grammatology. (Trans.) Gayatri Chakravorty Spivak. Baltimore & London: Johns Hopkins University Press.

Derrida, J. (1982). Margins of Philosophy. Chicago: University of Chicago Press.

Dickson, D. (1977). Politics of Alternative Technology. New York: Universe Publisher.

Dirlik, A. (1999). "Is There History after Eurocentrism? Globalism, Postcolonialism and the Disavowal of History". In Cultural Critique. 42:1-34

Doyle, E.M. and Floyd, V.H. (eds.) (1973). Studies in Interpretation. Atlanta, G.A.: Rodopi.

Dunn, R.G. (1998). Identity Crises: A Social Critique of Postmodernity. Minnesota: University of Minnesota Press.

Dyson, E. (1997). Release 2.0. New York: Broadway.

Dyson, E. (1998). Release 2.1: A Design for Living in the Digital Age. New York: Broadway.

Eagleton, T. (1996). The Illusions of Postmodernism. London: Wiley.

Eagleton, T. (2003). After Theory. London: Penguin Books.

Eshelman, R. (2009). Performatism, or the End of Postmodernism. Aurora CO.:Davies Group.

Feldman, A. (2013). Dramas of the Past on the Twentieth-Century Stage: In History's Wings. London: Routledge.

Ferguson, N. (2003). Empire: The Rise and Demise of the British World Order and the Lessons for Global Power. New York: Basic Books.

Ferguson, N. (2008). Empire: How Britain Made the Modern World. London: Penguin Books.

Ferro, M. (1997). Colonization: A Global History. London: Routledge.

Festinger, L. (1962). A Theory of Cognitive Dissonance. Stanford: Stanford University Press.

Festinger, L. (1964). Conflict, Decision, and Dissonance - Volume 3. Stanford: Stanford University Press.

Feuer, L.S. (1989). Imperialism and the Anti-Imperialist Mind. New Brunswick, N.J.: Transaction Publishers, 1989.

Fischer, G. and Greiner, B. (eds.) (2007). The Play Within the Play: The Performance of Meta-theatre. New York: Rodopi.

Foucault, M. (2002). The Order of Things. London: Routledge.

Foucault, M. (2004). Society Must be Defended. (trans.) David Marcey. Lectures at the College de France 1975-1976. London: Penguin.

Fuchs, E. (1996). The Death of Character: Perspectives on Theater after Modernism. Indiana: Indiana University Press.

Gabriel, B. and Ilcan, S. (2004). Postmodernism and the Ethical Subject. Montreal & Ontario: McGill-Queen's Press – MQUP.

Gennep, A. (1960) The Rites of Passage. M.B. Vizedon and G.L. Caffee (trans.). London: Routledge and Kegan Paul. First published in 1909.

Gennep, A.V. 1977. The Rites of Passage. London: Oxford University Press.

Gerstle, C.A. and Milner, A.C. (1995). Recovering the Orient: Artists, Scholars, Appropriations. Newark, N.J.: Harwood Academic Publishers.

Giddens, A. (1993). New Rules of Sociological Method: A Positive Critique of Interpretative Sociologies. Stanford, CA: Stanford University Press.

Gillingham, J. (1992). "The Beginnings of English Imperialism". Journal of Historical Sociology. vol. 5, no. 4, pp. 392-409, 1992.

Guerlac, S. (2000). Literary Polemics. Stanford: Leland Stanford Junior University Publications.

Gutleben, C. (2002). Nostalgic Postmodernism: The Victorian Tradition and the Contemporary British Novel. Atlanta, G.A.: Rodopi.

Habermas, J. (1990). The Philosophical Discourse of Modernity. Manchester: MIT Press.

Habermas, J. (1990). The Philosophical Discourse of Modernity: Twelve Lectures. (trans.) Frederick G. Lawrence. Massachusetts: MIT.

Haferkamp, H. and Smelser, N.J. (eds.) (1992). Social Change and Modernity. California: University of California Press.

Hall, C. (2002). Civilising Subjects: Metropole and Colony in the English Imagination 1830-1867. Chicago: The University of Chicago Press.

Haney, W.S. II (1990). "Soyinka's Ritual Drama: Unity, Postmodernism, and the Mistake of the Intellect". Research in African Literatures. Vol. 21, No. 4 (Winter, 1990), pp. 33-54.

Haney, W.S. II (2008). Integral Drama: Culture, Consciousness and Identity (Consciousness, Literature & the Arts). Atlanta, G.A.: Rodopi.

Harvey, D. (1991). The Condition of Postmodernity: An Enquiry into the Origins of Cultural Change. Oxford: Blackwell Publishers.

Hassan, I.H. (1982). The Dismemberment of Orpheus: Toward a Postmodern Literature. London: The University of Wisconsin Press.

Hassan, I.H. (1987). The Postmodern Turn: Essays in Postmodern Theory and Culture. Ohio: Ohio State University Press.

Hassan, I.H. (2000). From Postmodernism to Postmodernity. London: Earthspace Visual Arts Centre.

Hazell, C. (2011). Alterity: The Experience of the Other. Bloomington: AuthorHouse.

Hegarty, P. (2004). Jean Baudrillard: Live Theory. London: Continuum.

Hillman, J. (1960). Emotion: A Comprehensive Phenomenology of Theories And Their Meanings for Therapy. London: Routledge.

Hoffmann, G. (2005). From Modernism to Postmodernism: Concepts and Strategies of Postmodern American Fiction. New York: Rodopi.

Hooti, N. (2011). Oscillation between Modernism to Postmodernism in Shakespeare's Hamlet. In Theory and Practice in Language Studies, Vol. 1, No. 4, pp. 327-336, April 2011.

Howard, D. (1981). "The Politics of Modernism: From Marx to Kant". In Philosophy & Social Criticism December 1981 vol. 8 no. 4. (pp. 360-386).

Huddart, D. (2006). Homi K. Bhabha. Oxon: Routledge.

Hunt, L. (2009). The Making of the West: Volume C. Bedford: St. Martin.

Hutcheon, L. (1980). Narcissistic Narrative: The Metafictional Paradox. Ontario: Wilfrid Laurier University Press.

Hutcheon, L. (1988). A Poetics of Postmodernism: History, Theory, Fiction. London: Routledge.

Hutcheon, L. (1989). The Politics of Postmodernism. London: Routledge.

Hutcheon, L. (1994). Irony's Edge: The Theory and Politics of Irony. London: Routledge.

Inda, J. and Rosaldo, R. (2008). "Introduction: A World in Motion". In Inda, J. and Rosaldo, R. (eds.) The Anthropology of Globalization. Oxford: Blackwell.

Israel, J. (2001). Radical Enlightenment: Philosophy and the Making of Modernity 1650–1750. Oxford, Oxford University Press.

Israel, J. (2006). Enlightenment Contested: Philosophy, Modernity, and the Emancipation of Man, 1670–1752. Oxford: Oxford University Press.

Jameson, F. (1991). Postmodernism, Or, The Cultural Logic of Late Capitalism. Durham: Duke University Press.

Jencks, C. (2007). Critical Modernism: Where is Post-Modernism Going What is Post-Modernism. London: Wiley.

Jenkins, H. (2005). Textual Poachers: Television Fans and Participatory Culture (Studies in Culture and Communication). New York: New York University Press.

Jenkins, H. (2006a). Convergence Culture: Where Old and New Media Collide. New York: New York University Press.

Jenkins, H. (2006b). Fans, Bloggers and Gamers: Essays on Participatory Culture. New York: New York University Press.

Jenkins, H. (2013). Spreadable Media: Creating Value and Meaning in a Networked Culture (Postmillennial Pop). New York: New York University Press.

Jernigan, D.K. (2008). Drama and the Postmodern: Assessing the Limits of Metatheatre. Amherst, N.Y.: Cambria Press.

Jeyifo, B. (1990). "The Nature of Things: Arrested Decolonization and Critical Theory". Research in African Literatures 21.1 (1990): 33–48.

Jeyifo, B. (2004). Wole Soyinka. Cambridge: Cambridge University Press.

Jeyifo, B. (ed.) 2001. Perspectives on Wole Soyinka. Freedom and Complexity. Mississippi: University Press of Mississippi

Johnston, R.J., et. al. (eds.) (2009). The Dictionary of Human Geography. London: Blackwell.

Johnstone, K. (2012) Impro: Improvisation and the Theatre. New York: Routledge.

Kellner, D. (1994). Baudrillard: A Critical Reader. London: Wiley.

Khapoya, V.B. (2010). The African Experience: An Introduction. London: Longman.

Kim, S.J. (2009). Critiquing Postmodernism in Contemporary Discourses of Race. New York: Palgrave Macmillan, 2009

Kirby, A. (2007). "The Death of Postmodernism And Beyond". New Statesman, 19 March 2007, 48.http://philosophynow.org/issues/58/The_Death_of_Po stmodernism_And_Beyond. Retrieved 17 July, 2013.

Kirby, A. (2009). Digimodernism: How New Technologies Dismantle the Postmodern and Reconfigure our Culture. London: Continuum.

Knapp, R., Morris, M. and Wolf, S. (2011). The Oxford Handbook of The American Musical. Oxford: Oxford University Press.

Kraidy, Marwan (2005). Hybridity, or the Cultural Logic of Globalization. Philadelphia, PA: Temple University Press. pp. 1–23.

Kristeva, J. (1982). Powers of Horror: An Essay on Abjection. (Trans.) Leon S. Roudiez. New York: Colombia University Press.

Kul-Want, C. (2010). Philosophers on Art from Kant to the Postmodernists: A Critical Reader. New York: Colombia University Press.

Lacan, J. (1988). The Seminar of Jaques Lacan 1. Cambridge: Cambridge University Press.

Lacan, J. (2004). The Four Fundamental Concepts of Psychoanalysis. London: Hogarth Press.

Lehmann, H-T. (2006). Postdramatic Theatre. (Trans.) Karen Jurs-Munby. Oxon: Routledge.

Levinas, E. (1991). Otherwise than Being, or Beyond Essence. (Trans) . Alphonso Lingis Dordrecht and Boston, MA: Kluwer Academic Publishers.

Levinas, E. (1994).Outside the Subject. Stanford: Stanford University Press.

Levinas, E. (2003).Humanism of the Other. Illinois: University of Illinois Press.

Lipovetsky, G. and Charles, S. (2005). Hypermodern Times. Themes for the 21st Centrury. London: Wiley.

Lowe, K. (2012). Savage Continent: Europe in the Aftermath of World War Two London: Viking.

Lyotard, J. F. (2011). Discourse Figure. (Trans.) Anthony Hudek and Mary Lydon. Minnesota: University of Minnesota.

Lyotard, J.F. (1984). The Postmodern Condition: A Report on Knowledge. Manchester: Manchester University Press.

Macey, D. (2004). Michel Foucault. London: Reaktion Books.

MacIntyre, A. (1990). Three Rival Versions of Moral Enquiry: Encyclopaedia, Genealogy, and Tradition. Notre Dame, IN: University of Notre Dame Press.

MacKay, M. (2007). Modernism and World War II. Cambridge: Cambridge University Press.

Malkin, J.R. (1999). Memory-Theater and Postmodern Drama. Michigan: University of Michigan Press.

Mariani, U. (2008). Living Masks: The Achievement of Pirandello. Toronto: University of Toronto Press.

Marrouchi, M. (2004). Edward Said at the Limits. Albany: State University of New York Press.

Mason, F. (2007). The A to Z of Postmodernist Literature and Theater. Plymouth: Scarecrow Press.

McLuhan, M. (2001). Understanding Media: The Extensions of Man. London: Routledge.

Memmi, A. (2003). The Colonizer and the Colonized. London: Earthscan Publications.

Merrin, W. (2005). Baudrillard and the Media: A Critical Introduction. Cambridge: Polity Press.

Meyer-Dinkgräfe, M. (2005). Theatre And Consciousness: Explanatory Scope And Future Potential. Bristol: Intellect Books.

Michelfelder, D.P. and Palmer, R.E. (1989). Dialogue and Deconstruction: The Gadamer-Derrida Encounter. New York: State University of New York Press.

Moody, A.D. (ed.) (1994). The Cambridge Companion to T.S. Eliot. Cambridge: Cambridge University Press.

Morris, R.C. (2010). Can the Subaltern Speak? Reflections on the History of an Idea. New York: Colombia University Press.

Morton, S. (2007). Gayatri Spivak: Ethics, Subalternity and the Critique of Postcolonial Reason. Cambridge: Polity Press.

Mukherjee, A.P. (1990). "Whose Post-Colonialism and Whose Postmodernism?". In World Literature Written in English. Volume 30, Issue 2, 1990. pp 1-9.

Mwangi, E.M. (2009). Africa Writes Back to Self. Albany: State University of New York Press.

Needham, J. (1990). A selection from the writings of Joseph Needham. (ed.) Mansel Davies. Jefferson, N.C.: McFarland & Company Incorporated Pub, 1 Jan 1990

Nicol, B. (2009). The Cambridge Introduction to Postmodern Fiction. Cambridge: Cambridge University Press.

Okafor, D. (ed.) (2001). Meditations on African Literature. Westport, CT.: Greenwood Press.

Oksala, J. (2005). Foucault on Freedom. Cambridge: Cambridge University Press.

Oliver, K. (1993). Ethics, Politics, and Difference in Julia Kristeva's Writings. London: Routledge.

Ong, W. (2002). Orality and Literacy: The Technologizing of the Word. New York: Routledge.

Osterhammel, J. (2005). Colonialism: A Theoretical Overview. (trans.) Shelley Frisch. Princeton, N.J.: Markus Weiner Publishers.

Outram, D. (1995). The Enlightenment. Cambridge: Cambridge University Press.

Outram,D. (2006). Panorama of the Enlightenment. Los Angeles: Getty Publications.

Pamatmat, M. (2007). Hyper-surrealism: A Successor to Postmodernism. California: California State University.

Perry, N. (1998). Hyperreality and Global Culture. London: Routledge.

Peters, G. (2009). The Philosophy of Improvisation. Chicago: University of Chicago Press.

Pettit, Philip (1975). The Concept of Structuralism: A Critical Analysis. California: University of California Press.

Pierce, D. and Voogd, P.J. (eds.) (1996). Laurence Sterne in Modernism and Postmodernism. Atlanta, G.A.: Rodopi.

Pieterse, Jan N. (2003). Globalization and Culture. Global Mélange. Plymouth: Rowman & Littlefield.

Pieterse, Jan N. (2004). Globalization or Empire. New York: Routledge.

Pizzato, M. (1998). Edges of Loss: From Modern Drama to Postmodern Theory. Michigan: Michigan University Press.

Potter, R.A. (1995). Spectacular Vernaculars: Hip-Hop and the Politics of Postmodernism. Albany: State University of New York.

Rademarcher, J.W. (1996). "Totalized (Auto)Biography as Fragmented Intertextuality – Shakespeare – Sterne – Joyce". In Pierce, D. and Voogd, P.J. (eds.) (1996). Laurence Sterne in Modernism and Postmodernism. Atlanta, G.A.: Rodopi.

Rengger, N. and Hoffman, M. (1992). "Modernity, Postmodernism and International Relations". In Doherty,

J., et al. (eds.) (1992). Postmodernism in the Social Sciences. London: Macmillan.

Robinson, M. (2009). The Cambridge Companion to August Strindberg. Cambridge: Cambridge University Press.

Rodney, W. (1973) How Europe Underdeveloped Africa. Dar-Es-Salam: East African Publishers.

Ronan, C.A. (1995). The Shorter Science and Civilisation in China: 5. Cambridge: Cambridge University Press.

Roose-Evans, J. (1970). Experimental Theatre: From Stanislavsky to Peter Brook. London: Routledge & Kegan Paul.

Rosso, S. and Springer, C. (1983). A Correspondence with Umberto Eco. Genova-Bologna-Binghamton-Bloomington August-September, 1982 March-April, 1983. Vol. 12, No. 1 (Autumn, 1983), pp. 1-13

Russell, B. (1946). A History of Western Philosophy. London: George Allen & Unwin

Said, E.W. (1978). Orientalism: Western Conceptions of the Orient. London: Routledge & Kegan Paul.

Said, E.W. (2001). Reflections on Exile: And Other Literary and Cultural Essays. London: Granta Publications.

Samuels, R. (2010). New Media, Cultural Studies, and Critical Theory After Postmodernism: Automodernity from Zizek to Laclau. London: Palgrave Macmillan.

Sassower, R. (2013). Digital Exposure: Postmodern Postcapitalism. London: Palgrave Macmillan.

Saussure, F. (1959). Course in General Linguistics. (trans.) Wade Baskin. New York: Philosophical Library.

Schmid, H. and Kesteren, A.V. (eds.) (1984). Semiotics of Drama and Theatre: New Perspectives in the Theory of Drama and Theatre. Herndon, VA.: John Benjamins.

Schmidt, K. (2005). The Theater of Transformation: Postmodernism in American Drama. Atlanta, G.A.: Rodopi.

Scholes, R.E. (2006). Paradoxy of Modernism. Yale: Yale University Press.

Shephard, B. (2011). The Long Road Home: The Aftermath of the Second World War. London: Vintage Books.

Sheppard, R. (2000). Modernism – Dada – Postmodernism. Illinois: Northwester University Press.

Shillington, K. (2005). Encyclopedia of African History. New York: CRC Press.

Shillington, K. (2012). History of Africa. New York: Macmillian Publishers Limited.

Shohat, E and Stam, R. (1994). Unthinking Eurocentrism: Multiculturalism and the Media. London: Routledge.

Sim, S. (ed.) 2011. The Routledge Companion to Postmodernism. Oxon: Routledge.

Simon, D. (1998). "Rethinking (Post)modernism, Postcolonialism and Posttraditionalism: South-North Perspectives". In Environment and Planning D: Society and Space, 16(2): pp. 219-245.

Sinha, M. (2006). Specters of Mother India: The Global Restructuring of an Empire. Durham, N.C.: Duke University Press.

Slocombe, W. (2006). Nihilism and the Sublime Postmodern: The (Hi) Story of a Difficult Relationship. London: Routledge.

Smith, A. (1998). Julia Kristeva: Speaking The Unspeakable. London: Pluto Press.

Smith, H. and Dean, R.T. (1997). Improvisation, Hypermedia and the Arts Since 1945. London: Routledge.

Sokal, A. (2010). Beyond the Hoax: Science, Philosophy and Culture. Oxford: Oxford University Press.

Sokal, A. and Bricmont, J. (1999). Fashionable Nonsense: Postmodern Intellectuals' Abuse of Science. London: Picador.

Soyinka, W. (1999). Plays 2. London: Methuen.

Spivak, G.C. (1988). "Can the Subaltern Speak?" In Marxism and the Interpretation of Culture. (eds.) Cary Nelson and Lawrence Grossberg. Illinois: University of Illinois. (pp. 271-313).

Spivak, G.C. (1998). In Other Worlds: Essays in Cultural Politics. Oxon: Routledge.

Spivak, G.C. (1999). A Critique of Postcolonial Reason: Toward a History of the Vanishing Present. Havard: Havard University Press.

Sturrock, J. (1979). Structuralism and Since: from Lévi Strauss to Derrida: Introduction. Oxford: Oxford University Press.

Szakolczai, A. (2003). Reflexive Historical Sociology. London: Routledge.

Taylor, V.E. and Winquist, C.E. (2003). Encyclopedia of Postmodernism. London: Routledge.

Thomson, P. and Sacks, G. (2006). The Cambridge Companion to Brecht. Cambridge: Cambridge University Press.

Tiffin, H. (1988). "Post-Colonialism, Post-Modernism and the Rehabilitation of Post-Colonial History". In The Journal of Commonwealth Literature March 1988 vol. 23 no. 1 pp. 169-181.

Travers, M. (2006). European Literature from Romanticism to Postmodernism: A Reader in Aesthetic Practice. London: Continuum.

Turnbull, C. (1990) 'Liminality: A Synthesis of Subjective and Objective Experience.' in Richard Schechner and Willa Appel (eds.). By Means of Performance, Vol. 5. Cambridge: Cambridge University Press, pp. 50-81.

Turner, V. (1957) Schism and Continuity in an African Society: A Study of Ndembu Village Life. Manchester: Manchester University Press.

Turner, V. (1969). The Ritual Process. London: Penguin.

Turner, V. (1982) From Ritual to Theatre: The Human Seriousness of Play. New York: PAJ Publications.

Turner, V. (1984) 'Liminality and the Performance Genres.' in John J. MacAloon (ed.) Rite, Drama, Festival, Spectacle: Rehearsals Toward a Theory of Cultural Performance. Philadelphia: Institute for the Study of Human Issues.

Turner, V. (1987) The Anthropology of Performance. New York: PAJ Publications.

Vermeulen, T. and Akker, R. (2010). "Notes on Metamodernism". Journal of Aesthetics & Culture, Vol. 2, 2010 DOI: 10.3402/jac.v1i0.5677

Wagner, P. (2001). Theorizing Modernity: Inescapability and Attainability in Social Theory. London: SAGE.

Wagner, P. (2008). Modernity as Experience and Interpretation - A New Sociology of Modernity. Cambridge: Cambridge University Press.

Wagner, P. (2012). Modernity. Understanding the Present. Cambridge: Cambridge University Press.

Warraq, I. (2007). Defending the West: A Critique of Edward Said's Orientalism. London: Prometheus Books.

Wilkie, R. (2011). The Digital Condition: Class and Culture in the Information Network. New York: Fordham University Press.

Williams, P.J. and Chrisman, L. (1994). Colonial Discourse and Post-colonial Theory: A Reader. New York: Colombia University Press.

Wright, E. (1989). Postmodern Brecht: A Re-presentation. London: Routledge.

Yordon, J.E. (1997). Experimental Theatre: Creating and Staging Texts. Long Grove, IL: Waveland Press.

All the Titles in the Critical Mini-series on the Theatre of Wole Soyinka

ISBN   **Title**

978-0-9929618-4-8   The Theatre of Wole Soyinka: The Man, The Myth and the Meta-myth (Paperback)

978-0-9929618-5-5   The Theatre of Wole Soyinka: Modernism and Liminality (Paperback)

978-0-9929618-6-2   The Theatre of Wole Soyinka: Postmodernism and Postcolonialism (Paperback)

978-0-9929618-7-9   The Theatre of Wole Soyinka: Metamodernism, Myth and Ritual (Paperback)

978-0-9929618-8-6   The Theatre of Wole Soyinka: The Fall of Community and Society (Paperback)

978-0-9929618-9-3   The Theatre of Wole Soyinka: Performing Culture (Paperback)

www.ingramcontent.com/pod-product-compliance
Lightning Source LLC
Chambersburg PA
CBHW061431050726
47593CB00006B/2301